Living and Dying with the King James Bible

by
Harold R. Eberle

Worldcast Publishing
Yakima, Washington, USA

Living and Dying with the King James Bible

© 2010 by Harold R. Eberle

Worldcast Publishing
P.O. Box 10653
Yakima, WA 98909-1653
(509) 248-5837
www.worldcastpublishing.com
office@worldcastpublishing.com

ISBN 1-882523-36-8
Cover by Lynette Brannan

ALL RIGHTS RESERVED

No part of this publication may be reproduced, stored in a retrieval system, or transmitted in any form or by any means—electronic, mechanical, photocopy, recording, or otherwise—without the express prior permission of Worldcast Publishing Company, with the exception of brief excerpts in magazine articles and/or reviews.

Requests for translating into other languages should be addressed to Worldcast Publishing.

Printed in the United States of America.

Table of Contents

Introduction..1
1. The Historic Development of Our Bible............................3
2. KJV Was Based on the Bishops' Bible..............................6
3. KJV Referenced Inferior Manuscripts..............................6
4. A Host of Supporting Documents Today..........................9
5. The "Authorized" King James Version............................10
6. Political Pressures on the KJV Translators....................11
7. Manipulated Support for the Institutional Church........12
8. Manipulated Support for Authoritative Government....15
9. Too Condemning and Too Negative.................................16
10. Overemphasizes the Wickedness of Humanity.............17
11. Careless Mistakes in Verb Tenses..................................19
12. Serious Mistakes in Verb Tenses...................................20
13. Numerous Mistakes in Verb Tenses..............................22
14. No More Time?..24
15. Hades Is Not Hell..25
16. Jesus Descended into Hades, Not Hell..........................27
17. Jesus Preached in Hades..28
18. Hell Is Eternal Judgment...30
19. Women in the Ministry...32
20. Isaiah 14 Is Not About Satan...32
21. Holy Ghost Confusion in the KJV..................................36
22. God Did Not Create Evil...38
23. God Is Spirit..39
24. Man Is Not "a Spirit"...40
25. Animals Have Souls..42
26. "The" Root of All Evil..43
27. Does Not Allow for Ongoing Research...........................44
28. The Trinitarian Statement in the KJV..........................44
29. Why Is All of This Important?.......................................47
30. Unreadable to the Modern Mind....................................49
Conclusion...51

Introduction

The *King James Version* (KJV) has been a gift of God to the Body of Christ. It has been the standard of truth and inspiration which has stabilized the Protestant Church and blessed millions of people. But someone needs to say it: the KJV is an inferior translation. I will show you this in the pages to follow.

Of course, hearing anything negative about the KJV is going to be difficult for many Christians. They have spent their lives reading and studying the words of God as recorded on those holy pages. Many have been taught that the KJV is the only reliable version. Some have thought of it as God's true Word. Many churches will allow no other version to be read from their pulpits. English-speaking Christians across the world have memorized its sacred words, fed on its beauty and cherished its treasures.

I referred to "English-speaking Christians" because most of the world cannot read the KJV. They don't speak or read English.

Concerning this, I had an eye-opening experience a few years ago as I was teaching in a church in Tel Aviv, Israel. My words were being translated into the language of my Hebrew-speaking listeners. When I read from the Old Testament I commented that I was reading from my favorite English translation. My interpreter interrupted me and said that he would read from the Hebrew version. Suddenly it was obvious that my English version—no matter what English version I was using—was inferior to the original Hebrew Old Testament which each of those people sitting in front of me held in their hands.

The Old Testament was originally written in Hebrew and the New Testament was originally written in Greek.[1] No matter what version or translation we use today, it will

---

[1] Some small sections were written in Aramaic.

never be as accurate as the originals. However, we should use a version in our own language which is as close as possible to the original writings. Once the KJV was the most accurate translation available to English speakers. That is no longer true.

In order to show this in the following pages, I will compare the KJV to several other Bible translations, but primarily I will refer to the *New American Standard Version* (NASV). I am not trying to direct people to embrace the NASV. There are several excellent modern translations available today, but I needed to choose one translation so I could easily make comparisons to the KJV. The NASV is commonly used by English-speaking Bible College teachers and it is considered by scholars to be the most accurate word-by-word translation in the English language.

The *New International Version* (NIV) is also an excellent and very popular modern version. The translators of the NIV attempted to develop a version more easily readable than the NASV and they succeeded by translating phrase-by-phrase rather than word-by-word. Today the NIV is very often used when reading publicly from church pulpits because of its ease and understandability, while the NASV is used for serious personal study, along with the original languages.

I recommend people read the version through which God speaks to them. Throughout the years God has stirred in the hearts of gifted individuals to translate His precious Word and they have done so to the best of their abilities. God will direct His children to read His Word in a translation that reaches their heart and transforms their life. If the KJV speaks to you, then continue meditating on its treasures. However, you should be aware of some of its weaknesses and errors which more modern translations have corrected.

1) The Historic Development of Our Bible

Some proponents of the KJV will say, "If it was good enough for Paul, it is good enough for me!" Of course, they are simply expressing their loyalty to the KJV, but some people whom I have met actually believe that Paul used the KJV. In reality, Paul lived over 1500 years before the KJV came into existence, and he didn't speak English. To make it clear for everyone, a short history of the development of our Bible will help.

Before the KJV was produced in 1611, there were several translations in usage; the most noted are as follows:

> 1. The Latin translation, called the *Vulgate,* was produced by Jerome (347-420) and became the standard of Western Christianity up until the Protestant Reformation in the Sixteenth Century.
>
> 2. The first known translation into the English language was produced by John Wycliffe in 1380.
>
> 3. William Tyndale produced another version in the English language in 1526.
>
> 4. Luther had a Bible produced in German in the 1530's, but I will not speak further about this version since it was not in English.
>
> 5. In 1541, King Henry VIII had an English Bible produced, called the *Great Bible.*
>
> 6. The *Geneva Bible* was produced under John Calvin's oversight in 1560.

Living and Dying with the King James Bible

7. The *Bishops' Bible* was produced under the authority of the Church of England in 1568 and revised in 1572.

It was the revised version of the *Bishops' Bible* that became the base text for the *King James Version* (KJV), also called the *Authorized Version,* first printed in 1611.

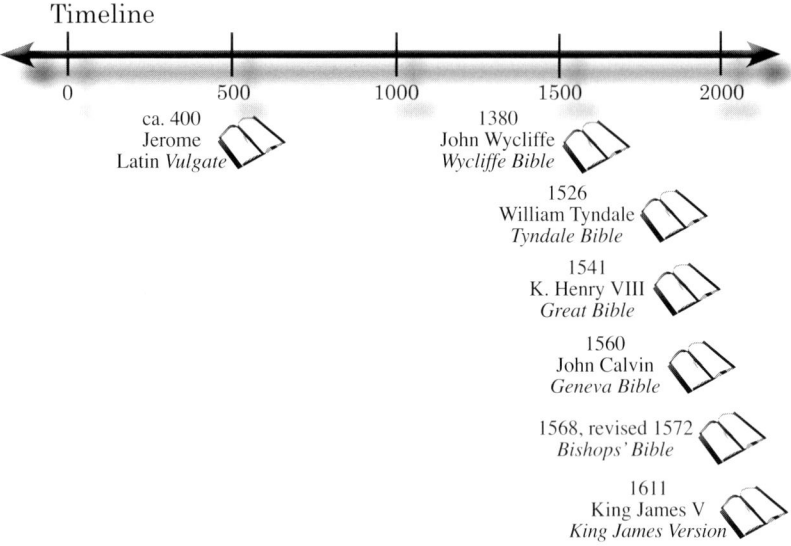

King James V had fifty-four scholars selected to develop the KJV (although only forty-seven were known to have taken part). These scholars were divided into six teams to translate different portions of the Bible. They met at Westminster, Cambridge and Oxford. King James had fifteen guidelines given to the scholars/translators. Those guidelines are listed below and you can refer back to this list as we discuss the most relevant guidelines in the pages to follow.

The Historic Development of Our Bible

King James' Guidelines

1. The ordinary Bible read in the Church, commonly called the Bishops Bible, to be followed, and as little altered as the Truth of the original will permit.

2. The names of the Prophets, and the Holy Writers, with the other Names of the Text, to be retained, as nigh as may be, accordingly as they were vulgarly used.

3. The Old Ecclesiastical Words to be kept, viz. the Word Church not to be translated Congregation & c.

4. When a Word hath divers Significations, that to be kept which hath been most commonly used by the most of the Ancient Fathers, being agreeable to the Propriety of the Place, and the Analogy of the Faith.

5. The Division of the Chapters to be altered, either not at all, or as little as may be, if Necessity so require.

6. No Marginal Notes at all to be affixed, but only for the explanation of the Hebrew or Greek Words, which cannot without some circumlocution, so briefly and fitly be expressed in the Text.

7. Such Quotations of Places to be marginally set down as shall serve for the fit Reference of one Scripture to another.

8. Every particular Man of each Company, to take the same Chapter or Chapters, and having translated or amended them severally by himself, where he thinketh good, all to meet together, confer what they have done, and agree for their Parts what shall stand.

9. As any one Company hath dispatched any one Book in this Manner they shall send it to the rest, to be considered of seriously and judiciously, for His Majesty is very careful in this Point.

10. If any Company, upon the Review of the Book so sent, doubt or differ upon any Place, to send them Word thereof; note the Place, and withal send the Reasons, to which if they consent not, the Difference to be compounded at the general Meeting, which is to be of the chief Persons of each Company, at the end of the Work.

11. When any Place of special Obscurity is doubted of, Letters to be directed by Authority, to send to any Learned Man in the Land, for his Judgement of such a Place.

12. Letters to be sent from every Bishop to the rest of his Clergy, admonishing them of this Translation in hand; and to move and charge as many skilful in the Tongues; and having taken pains in that kind, to send his particular Observations to the Company, either at Westminster, Cambridge, or Oxford.

13. The Directors in each Company, to be the Deans of Westminster, and Chester for that Place; and the King's Professors in the Hebrew or Greek in either University.

14. These translations to be used when they agree better with the Text than the Bishops Bible: Tyndale's, Matthew's, Coverdale's, Whitchurch's, Geneva.

15. Besides the said Directors before mentioned, three or four of the most Ancient and Grave Divines, in either of the Universities, not employed in Translating, to be assigned by the vice-Chancellor, upon Conference with the rest of the Heads, to be Overseers of the Translations as well Hebrew as Greek, for the better observation of the 4th Rule above specified.

2) KJV Was Based on the Bishops' Bible

The first guideline given to King James' scholars was:

> 1. The ordinary Bible read in the Church, commonly called the Bishops Bible, to be followed, and as little altered as the Truth of the original will permit.

The scholars who developed the KJV obeyed this first guideline and, therefore, followed the *Bishops' Bible*. To verify this, all one needs to do is read the preface written in the first edition of the KJV (1611) which states that their purpose was not "to make a new translation...but to make a good one better." The "good one" to which they referred was the *Bishops' Bible*.

Knowing this, we must question the statement which is commonly written in the introductory pages of modern KJV Bibles:

> *Translated out of the original tongues and with previous translations diligently compared and revised self-pronouncing.*

This statement is not entirely accurate. The original translators used Greek and Hebrew manuscripts to improve the *Bishops' Bible*, but they openly stated that the KJV was a revision of an earlier translation. They obeyed King James on this issue because to do otherwise would have put their lives at risk.

3) KJV Referenced Inferior Manuscripts

In revising the *Bishops' Bible*, the KJV translators referenced Hebrew and Greek manuscripts. For the New Testament, they

KJV Referenced Inferior Manuscripts

referenced the *Textus Receptus,* which was first published in 1516 by the Dutch Catholic scholar and humanist Desiderius Erasmus. To develop the *Textus Receptus*, Erasmus compiled six Greek manuscripts all dated from the Twelfth Century or later.

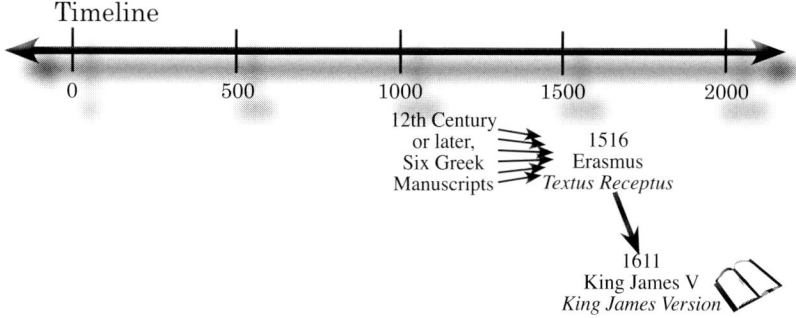

It is important to note the dates of those Greek manuscripts, because they were developed over 1,000 years after the original New Testament writings. Therefore, it would be wrong for us to think that the KJV's introductory phrase, "Translated out of the original tongues," meant that the KJV was translated out of or even referenced the original writings of the New Testament. That simply is not true.

For comparison's sake, we can note that most modern New Testament translations rely primarily on two manuscripts, *Codex Vaticanus* and *Codex Sinaiticus*, both of which are dated from the Fourth Century.

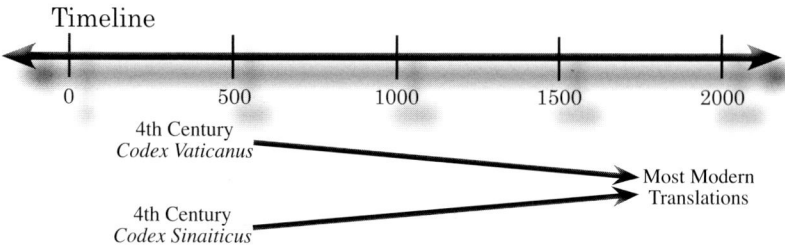

7

Living and Dying with the King James Bible

Why are these time differences important? Because manuscripts did not last very long, and so they had to be transcribed over and over again. The more time that passed, the more times they would have been transcribed, and hence, the more opportunities for mistakes to be made. This is especially true because scribes in the early Middle Ages took some freedom to add comments or change some wording to make things read as they thought they should read.

The original New Testament writings were produced in the First Century. Since the *Codex Vaticanus* and *Codex Sinaiticus* were both completed by the 300's, the transcribers may have had access to the original writings or, at the very least, writings that had been transcribed very few times. In contrast, over 1,000 years passed between the original New Testament writings and when the manuscripts used for the *Textus Receptus* were produced.

Even though advocates of the KJV do not like to admit it, the earlier Greek manuscripts (*Codex Vaticanus* and *Codex Sinaiticus*) used to produce most modern Bible translations are more reliable and accurate to the original, than the later Greek manuscript (*Textus Receptus*) used to correct the KJV.

Even Erasmus, who developed the *Textus Receptus,* did not consider it reliable. He recognized that the scribes who transcribed the Greek texts over and over again often made mistakes. Concerning the work of the scribes, He wrote:

> "But one thing the facts cry out, and it can be clear, as they say, even to a blind man, that often through the translator's clumsiness or inattention the Greek has been wrongly rendered; often the true and genuine reading has been corrupted by ignorant scribes, which we see happen every

day, or altered by scribes who are half-taught and half-asleep."[2]

In spite of Erasmus' doubts about the reliability of the Greek manuscripts available to him (and in spite of the 1,000+ years' gap), modern proponents of the KJV claim that the *Textus Receptus* is the most reliable record we have of the original New Testament writings.

In particular, there is a modern-day group called the King-James-Only Movement; they and a few others continue to support the validity of the *Textus Receptus* which was used to produce the KJV. Interestingly, most of the King-James-Only people are so fundamental in their own beliefs that they would never even consider Erasmus a true Christian if they knew his beliefs as a Roman Catholic priest.

The fact is that no modern school of textual scholarship continues to defend the superiority of the *Textus Receptus.*

4) A Host of Supporting Documents Today

Not only do the translators of the modern Bible versions use much older manuscripts, but they also have additional advantages over the KJV translators. Most importantly, they have available to them over 5,600 Greek (some dated as early as the Second Century) and 8,000 early Latin manuscripts of the New Testament. Modern translators use these to cross reference for accuracy of every word and phrase.

Today's abundance of early manuscripts makes the arguments of the King-James-Only-Movement foolish. They argue that the *Textus Receptus* is more accurate than the *Codex Vaticanus* and the *Codex Sinaiticus,* claiming that the two

---

[2] "Epistle 337" in *Collected Works of Erasmus,* vol. 3, p. 134.

earlier writings had been produced by unorthodox leaders who distorted the two *Codex* versions to support their own beliefs. That argument may have been reasonable when translators were only using these two *Codex* versions, but now they have over 5,600 Greek manuscripts. It is foolish to state that all the early manuscripts were distorted, while the *Textus Receptus* produced over 1,000 years later is perfect.

The abundance of early writings now available also allows modern translators to develop a better understanding of the ancient Greek language.

One further advantage which modern translators have is the availability of the writings of the Church fathers who lived in the First and Second Centuries. Some of those writings were available to the scholars/translators of the KJV, but today there are many more. Those Church fathers quoted extensively—over 80,000 verses—from the original writings of the New Testament Gospels and letters. It is difficult to underestimate the value of those quotations.

Modern proponents of the KJV like to defend its accuracy, but that is a difficult position to hold with integrity.

5) The "Authorized" King James Bible

Some advocates of the KJV will proudly point out that the KJV is the *Authorized Version*. In making this observation they are implying that the KJV is somehow authoritative or even divinely superior. In reality, it was the Church of England which authorized the KJV. The Church of England had previously authorized two other versions: the *Great Bible* and the *Bishops' Bible*. "Authorized" simply meant that the Church of England officially recognized it for use in public worship.

6) Political Pressures on the KJV Translators

At the time when the KJV was being developed, Europe was in a religious revolution. Approximately one-half of Europeans had left the Roman Catholic Church. Thousands of lives were lost in the related battles. Protestants wanted a version of the Bible which could be read in the language of the common people. They wanted a standard of truth, but some of their motivation was to have a version which made separation from the Roman Catholic Church and the pope justifiable. Kings also wanted a Bible that would bring peace and stability to their people.

Historians can identify these concerns in the guidelines which King James V gave to his scholars/translators. For example, the King's first guideline had to do with using the *Bishops' Bible* as a foundational text. A major reason for this was to steer the scholars away from using John Calvin's Bible. Calvin's Bible, called the *Geneva Bible*, was the most popular Bible being used by Protestants of that period. It had marginal notes which were anti-Catholic and with a strong Calvinistic bent. John Calvin had specific verses interpreted in a way that justified rebellion to political authority, and the marginal notes encouraged disobedience to kings. Knowing this, King James did not want his scholars borrowing from the *Geneva Bible*.

Nor did he want them to insert marginal notes like John Calvin did. This is one of the reasons that guideline number six forbade them from inserting any marginal notes except those necessary to clarify certain Hebrew and Greek terms.

Each of the guidelines may sound to us very reasonable and innocent, but the scholars of the period knew exactly what King James was demanding. They were not to make any of the same errors which John Calvin had made. Furthermore, the

11

scholars who developed the KJV were under intense social and political pressures. They were required to interpret key passages in ways that reveal the biases of those who commissioned them.

In the pages which follow, I will explain some of those biases and how they distorted the KJV from the original Hebrew and Greek manuscripts.

Note that most of my comments are also true of the *New King James Version* (NKJV). Some Christians have shifted from the KJV to the NKJV thinking that they have modernized but the NKJV has most of the errors which I describe below.

7) Manipulated Support for the Institutional Church

The third guideline which King James gave to his scholars/translators stated:

> 3. The Old Ecclesiastical Words to be kept, viz. the Word Church not to be translated Congregation & c.

When King James instructed the scholars to use "Old Ecclesiastical Words" such as "Church," he was saying to them that they must use words which support the institutional Church.

To see this, consider Hebrews 2:12 which says in the KJV:

> *...in the midst of the church will I sing praise unto thee.*

In contrast, the NASV says:

Manipulated Support for the Institutional Church

> *...in the midst of the congregation I will sing Your praise.*

In this verse, the Greek word translated as "church" in the KJV, and as "congregation" in the NASV, is *ekklesia*. The prefix, *ek*, means "out" and *klesia* means "called ones," so the word *ekklesia* literally refers to a group called out of the rest of humanity. During the New Testament times, this Greek word was used to refer to various types of groups. For example, in Acts 19:39, *ekklesia* refers to an official gathering of government officials; in Acts 19:32 and 41, it refers to a riotous mob. The point is that *ekklesia* was a common Greek word which could refer to various groups of people. But King James insisted that *ekklesia* be interpreted as Church rather than congregation when it referred to a group of Christians. This manipulation of words gave the support that King James wanted given to the institutional Church.

Giving further support to the institutional Church, the KJV translators used the title "bishop." For example, Philippians 1:1 says in the KJV (underlining added):

> *Paul and Timotheus, the servants of Jesus Christ, to all the saints in Christ Jesus which are at Philippi, with the <u>bishops</u> and deacons:*

In contrast, the NASV says,

> *Paul and Timothy, bond-servants of Christ Jesus, To all the saints in Christ Jesus who are in Philippi, including the <u>overseers</u> and deacons:*

What is the difference between bishops and overseers? "Bishop" is an official position in the institutional Church. Someone who only reads the KJV is going to think that the true Church must have bishops in leadership positions. In reality, *there was no office of bishop when the New Testament was written.* The title "bishop" was incorporated by the translators of the KJV to satisfy the demands of King James to support the institutional Church.

This issue is important to me, personally, because I believe that the Church is supposed to be structured around the fivefold ministry, that is, the ministries listed in Ephesians 4:11: apostles, prophets, evangelists, pastors and teachers.[3] As long as people only read the KJV and believe the Church should be organized around bishops, they are going to have a more difficult time seeing the benefit and biblical pattern of having apostles, prophets, evangelists, pastors and teachers. When we use the biblical term "overseer," it tends to be easier to see how a church leader may be gifted with any of the fivefold ministries. On the other hand, the term "bishop" designates an official position, a position which is complete in itself needing no further defining as apostle, prophet, etc. This distinction is worked out in the modern denominations which are structured after the bishop model. They tend to have a difficult time embracing any other model.

The KJV supports the institutional Church in other ways, but let me just mention one more. The KJV of Acts 12:4 tells us how Herod put Peter in prison, *"intending after Easter to bring him forth to the people."* Notice the word "Easter." There was no such day called Easter when the Book of Acts was written. Easter is an official holy day established by the Church several hundred years after the New Testament was completed. The original Greek manuscripts have the word, *pascha* which actually means Passover—as it is translated in most modern translations.

---

[3] I have explained this in another book, *The Complete Wineskin.*

8) Manipulated Support for Authoritarian Government

The KJV translators also manipulated words with the goal of reinforcing established authorities. Consider how the KJV translators talked about Church leaders "ruling over" the people. Hebrews 13:7 says in the KJV (underlining added):

Remember them which have the <u>rule over</u> you...

In contrast, the NASV translates these words more accurately using less heavy-handed terminology:

Remember those who <u>led</u> you...

Such overbearing terminology is used in other verses of the KJV as well:

Obey them that have the <u>rule over</u> you...
(Heb. 13:17, KJV)

Salute all that have the <u>rule over</u> you...
(Heb. 13:24, KJV)

Rather than referring to "those who rule over," other translations use words like "leaders" or "those who have oversight." The idea of "ruling over" is much stronger than "having oversight."

The point is that the translators of the KJV and NKJV used language which fostered the exercise of more authority than was intended by the original authors.

9) Too Condemning and Too Negative

Some passages in the KJV have been translated using terminology which is overly harsh and condemning. For example, Roman 8:1 says in the KJV:

> *There is therefore now no condemnation to them which are in Christ Jesus, who walk not after the flesh, but after the Spirit.*

In contrast, the NASV says:

> *Therefore there is now no condemnation for those who are in Christ Jesus.*

Notice that the last phrase—*"who walk not after the flesh, but after the Spirit"*—does not appear in the NASV, nor does it appear in most modern translations.

Why? The *Textus Receptus* included this phrase, whereas the older Greek manuscripts do not. This leads us to believe that the later scribes added it so as to make the passage say what they felt it should say.

Why is this important? The KJV is wrong in saying that the absence of condemnation is dependent upon the believer walking after the Spirit. We know from other Bible passages that the believer has been forgiven and God has promised *"to remember their sins no more"* (i.e., Heb. 8:12). There is no condemnation for any Christian; all Christians have a right to live their lives knowing that God's wrath has been removed from them.

10) Overemphasizes the Wickedness of Humanity

The KJV uses terminology which overemphasizes the wickedness of humanity. For example, Jeremiah 17:9 says in the KJV (underlining added):

> *The heart is deceitful above all things, and desperately <u>wicked</u>...*

The NASV translates the same verse as:

> *The heart is more deceitful than all else And is desperately <u>sick</u>...*

Is the human heart desperately *sick* or desperately *wicked*? There is a difference.

Christians who only read the KJV tend to use Jeremiah 17:9 as a condemnation of every human being on earth, claiming that all of us have desperately wicked hearts.

In reality, the context of Jeremiah 17:9 is making a contrast between a person with a good heart and those with an evil heart. If we read the preceding verses, we see that Jeremiah 17:5 and 6 talk about a person with an evil heart, while Jeremiah 17:7 and 8 talk about a person with a good heart.

The point of Jeremiah 17:9 is *not* that every human being has a desperately wicked heart. In fact, there are several verses in the Bible which talk about people—even non-Christians—who have a good heart. Not only do Jeremiah 17:7 and 8 tell us this, but Jesus explained how:

> *"The good man brings out of his good treasure what is good..."*
>
> (Matt. 12:35, NASV)

17

Jesus several times referred to people with good hearts. For example, He said that God causes the sun to rise on the evil and the good (Matt. 5:45). Further, He described Nathaniel before he was even a Christian, saying that in him *"there is no deceit"* (John 1:47). Not everyone has a deceitful heart.

This does not mean that some people are so good that they need no forgiveness of sins. That is not what I am saying. Everyone sins. Everyone needs the salvation which is only available through Jesus Christ. However, not everyone is as evil as the KJV leads one to believe.

This subject of how evil humanity is, is distorted in other passages in the KJV as well. That tendency was in keeping with the thought patterns of the Middle Ages and the Protestant Reformation. People in the Middle Ages thought of themselves as helplessly wicked. Further, the Reformers were trying to make the point that no one is good enough to get to heaven apart from Jesus. No one can be saved by good works. Indeed, everyone needs a Savior, but in trying to make this point, the leaders of the Protestant Reformation overemphasized humanity's sinfulness.

Jeremiah 17:9 is not a condemnation of every human being. As mentioned, the context is a contrast between a person with a good heart and a person with an evil heart. The emphasis in verse 9 is actually on the phrase, *"the heart is deceitful."* This deceitfulness is in the sense that the heart can rationalize sin. People are able to justify in their own heart their own actions. For this reason, the very next verse says, *"I, the Lord, search the heart..."* This brings the passage into its proper context, because people can rationalize their sins to themselves, but God sees through it all. The point is not that everyone is totally wicked. Some people have good hearts while others have evil hearts, but God sees all.

11) Careless Mistakes in Verb Tenses

The sinfulness of humanity is further exaggerated in the KJV because of the translators' negligence in preserving accurate verb tenses. For example, Isaiah 64:6 says in the KJV (underlining added):

> *But we <u>are</u> all as an unclean thing, and all our righteousnesses are as filthy rags...*

Many KJV advocates have taken this verse and applied it to all humanity, teaching that we all are unclean and all of our righteous deeds—all of the things we try do to please God—are rejected by God.

In reality, Isaiah 64:6 was written at a specific time in history referring to a specific group of people. Therefore, it is wrong to apply this verse to every human being throughout history. To see this, consider modern translations such as the NASV which says (underlining added):

> *For all of us <u>have become</u> like one who is unclean, And all our righteous deeds are like a filthy garment...*

Notice the tense of the verbs, *"have become."* This means the people were not always unclean, but they *had become* unclean.

Isaiah wrote this verse referring to his own people, the Jews. He was speaking about the condition of the Jews at a time when they were being taken out of Israel and exiled to Babylon. The Jews had been so rebellious to God that God was allowing them to be punished. The Jews were not always rejected by God. There was a time when they had God's favor. He once accepted their offerings and sacrifices. To confirm this, all we have to do is read one verse earlier:

> *You meet him who rejoices in doing righteousness...*
>
> (Is. 64:5)

God does not reject the righteous deeds of every human being. God loves it when a mother takes care of her children. He rejoices when a father works to provide for his family. In Acts 10:1-4 we read how God received the prayers of Cornelius, who was not even a Christian.

By the end of the Old Testament times, the Jewish people had been so rebellious for so long that God was no longer accepting their prayers or offerings. They "had become" unclean in God's eyes. They reached a state in which God was rejecting their righteous deeds.

This truth is difficult to see for those who only use the KJV because the translators were sometimes careless in accurately translating verb tenses.

12) Serious Mistakes in Verb Tenses

There are some passages in which a mistake in translating the verb tense does not alter the meaning of the passage, but there are others in which it makes a significant difference. For example, there are several passages in the Bible that talk about Christians dying with Christ or being crucified with Him (underlining added):

> *Knowing this, that our old man <u>is crucified</u> with him...*
>
> (Rom. 6:6, KJV)

> *I <u>am crucified</u> with Christ...*
>
> (Gal. 2:20, KJV)

Notice that both of these verses imply that the Christian is crucified right now—in the present tense—with Christ. This gives us the sense that we are to see ourselves as hanging on the cross with Jesus who hung on the cross 2,000 years ago.

In contrast, the NASV translates the verb tenses accurately from the original Greek language (underlining added):

> *knowing this, that our old self <u>was crucified</u> with Him...*
> (Rom. 6:6, NASV)
>
> *I <u>have been crucified</u> with Christ...*
> (Gal. 2:20, NASV)

Both of these verses show that the Christian *was* crucified or *has been* crucified with Christ. Therefore, it is not an ongoing experience for us. The Christian's death was accomplished at the cross 2,000 years ago.

This distinction makes a profound difference in how Christians understand the victorious life which is available to us in Jesus. Those who read the KJV tend to conclude that Christians should see themselves as hanging on the cross with Jesus. Those who read the NASV or any other modern translation which is careful with the Greek verb tenses will conclude that our death was something accomplished 2,000 years ago. Therefore, we do not have to *kill* ourselves today.

The concept of crucifying oneself or dying to oneself is a theme which is commonly discussed among Christian groups who primarily use the KJV. It fits well with the overemphasis which we already discussed about the wickedness of humanity. Since people see themselves as terrible, they can easily conclude that they should put themselves to death.

In reality, there is *no verse in the Bible that tells us or even implies that the Christian should kill or crucify himself or herself.* An accomplished work does not need to be repeated.

There is one verse, Roman 8:13, which talks about *"putting to death the deeds of the body."* This is part of the ongoing Christian life, but putting to death certain *deeds* is very different than putting to death *self*. The first is Scriptural, the second is not.

The difference between putting to death deeds and putting to death self is key to living the victorious Christian life. Let me be so bold as to say that if you do not know the difference, it is because you have been trained by Christians who rely too heavily on the KJV. For those interested in further study on this subject, I have written two books which offer clear explanations: *Jesus Came Out of the Tomb, So Can You* and *Grace, the Power to Reign*.

13) Numerous Mistakes in Verb Tenses

Some of the mistakes which the KJV translators made with verb tenses may have resulted from a lack of understanding the ancient Greek language. As explained earlier, the translators of KJV did not have the resources available to them that translators do today. Hence, they did not have an adequate understanding of the intricacies of the original languages. Other errors may have resulted from carelessness or simply not realizing how important it was to translate the exact meaning of a passage.

Here are a couple more passages with poorly translated verb tenses.

In the KJV of Matthew 16:19, Jesus says:

> *"and whatsoever thou shalt bind on earth shall be bound in heaven: and whatsoever thou shalt loose on earth shall be loosed in heaven."*

The NASV more accurately translates the verbs in their

Numerous Mistakes in Verb Tenses

proper tenses:

> *"and whatever you bind on earth shall have been bound in heaven, and whatever you loose on earth shall have been loosed in heaven."*

This distinction in verb tense is important because it reveals to us what comes first: the human action of binding on earth or the action of binding in heaven. In some Christian circles, confusion on this point has led to doctrinal error.

Another verse which reveals the KJV translators' carelessness in verb tenses and verb translations is Acts 2:47 (KJV):

> *...the Lord added to the church daily such as should be saved.*

In contrast, the NASV says:

> *...the Lord was adding to their number day by day those who were being saved.*

Notice how the KJV translators inserted the word "should." If you are theologically inclined, you will be able to think of how the insertion of this word can confuse the reader doctrinally. Ask yourself the question, "Is it possible to be added to the church before a person is saved?" According to the KJV it is.

Of all the modern translations, the NASV is known for interpreting the verbs from the original languages in their most accurate tenses. The NIV does a good job, but sometimes it changes the verb tenses from the original in order to make the passage easier to read. The NASV is more cumbersome, but truer to the original manuscripts.

14) No More Time?

In addition to the above mentioned problems with the KJV, there are specific passages which have led to significant theological errors.

To see this, consider Revelation 10:6 which says in the KJV that *"there should be time no longer..."* Some teachers have used this Bible passage to teach that there is no time in the spiritual realm or in heaven.

Yet, if time did not exist in the realm of the spirit, then there would be no time boundaries in that realm. If that were true, then demons could transcend time and go into your past to cause tremendous problems in your present and future life. Also, when judgment day comes and God throws Satan into the Lake of Fire, Satan could escape by moving outside the confines of time. The point is that demons are limited in time, even though they exist in the spirit realm.

Another fundamental characteristic of the spirit realm is that things change. For example, 2,000 years ago Jesus ascended far above all rule and authority. At that point in time He was enthroned above all the universe—things changed. If time did not exist in the spirit world, nothing could change. The obvious point is that things do change and, therefore, time does exist in the spirit realm.

Revelation 10:6 does not say that there will be no more time. This verse is actually speaking of impending destruction, and if we read the verse in its context, we understand it to mean that there will be no more time before the destruction recorded in Revelation chapters 5 through 10 is released. Recognizing this, many translations, such as the NASV translate the meaning of this verse more clearly by saying *"there will be delay no longer."*

To confirm this understanding, we can look at Hebrews 10:37 and Habakkuk 2:3, where similar terminology is used.

The point is that Revelation 10:6 was not saying that there will be no time in the spirit or in eternity, but rather there would be no more time before destruction comes.

This may seem like a small point, but the implications are profound. In fact, there are so many far-reaching implications that I wrote another book to explain how this idea is the foundation for maintaining a concept of God derived from the ancient Greek philosophers Plato and Aristotle. If you are interested enough to pursue this, you can read my book, entitled *Who Is God?*

15) Hades Is Not Hell

The KJV uses the word "hell" when it should use "hades." Because of this error, most users of the KJV do not even know the difference between hades and hell.

What is the difference? The English word "hades" is translated from the Greek word *hades*. Obviously, this should not be a difficult word to translate. Hades referred to the place of the dead, not hell. The place of the dead is where *all dead people* went in Old Testament times, before the death and resurrection of Jesus. Both good and bad people were held there. Hades was not a place where everyone was locked in suffering and pain, like hell is.

The NIV sometimes translates the Greek word *hades* as "the grave." This helps the reader to understand that hades is not hell. However, it can wrongly lead the reader to think of hades as nothing more than a grave, the physical site where a dead body lays. In reality, hades is a place where the souls of dead individuals await until they stand before Jesus at judgment day.

Verifying this is the Old Testament's use of the word, *sheol*. Psalm 16:10 (NASV) says:

> *For you will not abandon my soul to Sheol;*
> *Nor will You allow Your Holy One to undergo decay.*

This verse is repeated in the New Testament:

> *Because You will not abandon my soul to Hades,*
> *Nor allow Your Holy One to undergo decay.*
> (Acts 2:27, NASV)

Note that the word "sheol" in the Old Testament is replaced with "hades" in the New Testament. This is because the Old Testament was written in the Hebrew language while the New Testament was written in Greek. The Hebrew word *sheol* is equivalent to the Greek word *hades*. Both refer to the place where dead people—both good and bad—went before Jesus died and resurrected.

No one knows for certain what hades was like, but we can get a glimpse by reading Luke 16:19-31, where Jesus tells the story of Lazarus and the rich man who both died and went to hades. The story reveals that the rich man went to a region in hades called "the place of torment," while Lazarus went to a region in hades called "the bosom of Abraham." There was a chasm between the two regions, but the rich man was able to see across the chasm and see Lazarus who was far off. The place of torment was a place of anguish, but it would be wrong to equate that place with hell.

Hell is a word we properly use to refer to the place where wicked people will be sent only after the final judgment day. Jesus told about the final judgment day when,

> *"...all who are in the tombs will hear His voice, and will come forth; those who did the good deeds to a resurrection of life, those who committed the*

evil deeds to a resurrection of judgment"
(John 5:28-29, NASV)

Only after that future day of resurrection will all of humanity stand before Jesus and then the wicked will be sent to hell or what is also called the Lake of Fire (Rev. 20:14). We further know that hades and hell are different because Revelation 20:13 tells us that at the final judgment, even hades will be thrown into hell or into the Lake of Fire.

These distinctions are not made in the KJV. This leads readers to confuse hades and hell. It leads readers to think that evil people are immediately sent to hell once they die. In reality, they will suffer in the region of hades known as "the place of torment," but they will not be cast into hell—the eternal Lake of Fire—until the final judgment day.

What difference does it make? Not only is it wrong, but there are serious implications. Let me explain a few.

16) Jesus Descended into Hades, Not Hell

Once we have distinguished between hades and hell, we can consider how Jesus descended into hades during the period between His death and resurrection. Acts 2:27 reveals our Lord's words to the Father:

Because You will not abandon my soul to Hades, Nor allow Your Holy One to undergo decay.
(Acts 2:27, NASV)

The KJV wrongly says:

Because thou wilt not leave my soul in hell, neither wilt thou suffer thine Holy One to see corruption.
(Acts 2:27, KJV)

From this verse, Christians who rely only on the KJV, conclude that Jesus descended into hell between His death and resurrection. Typically, they understand hell to be a place of separation from God the Father, and therefore, they say that Jesus experienced total and complete separation from the Father.

Jesus may have experienced the pain of being forsaken by the Father when He hung on the cross and cried out, *"My God, My God, Why have You forsaken Me?"* But Jesus' sensation of being forsaken does not mean that God actually separated Himself from the Son. The very idea that the Father could separate Himself from the Son puts into question the Trinity, which tells us that the Father and Son are One.

17) Jesus Preached in Hades

Distinguishing between hades and hell also allows us to see how Jesus preached and then brought freedom to many of those in hades.

To see this, consider Peter's words which say that Jesus descended into hades (Acts 2:27, NASV). In another passage Peter explained how Jesus died and then preached to the people who were in hades: *"He went and made proclamation to the spirits now in prison"* (I Peter 3:19, NASV). Peter later says, *"For the gospel has for this purpose been preached even to those who are dead..."* (I Peter 4:6, NASV). This leads us to believe that between His death and resurrection, Jesus preached to and revealed Himself to the people in hades.

Paul further describes how Jesus came out of hades and *"He led captive a host of captives"* (Eph. 4:8, NASV). Yes, Jesus took a multitude of people out of hades with Him. Matthew describes how:

Jesus Preached in Hades

The tombs were opened, and many bodies of the saints who had fallen asleep were raised; and coming out of the tombs after His resurrection they entered the holy city and appeared to many.
(Matt. 27:52-53, NASV)

Many of those Old Testament saints appeared in Jerusalem before they ascended with Jesus into heaven.

This understanding is difficult, if not impossible, to come up with using only the KJV which confuses hades and hell. This is because it is difficult to conceive of Jesus leading people out of hell. It is also difficult to imagine the Old Testament saints like Abraham and Noah being held in hell, waiting for Jesus to come.

Once we understand that Jesus preached and presented Himself to those in hades between His death and resurrection, we get a new perspective of Paradise and the thief who died on the cross next to Jesus. Our Lord said to the thief, *"Today you shall be with Me in Paradise"* (Luke 23:43, NASV). Typically, KJV readers say that the thief was instantaneously saved and then taken to heaven upon his death. That cannot be true, because Jesus did not go to heaven right after His death. He went to hades.

We have more evidence that Jesus did not go to heaven right after His death, because after His resurrection He appeared to Mary and said, *"I have not yet ascended to the Father..."* (John 20:17, NASV).

How did Jesus go to Paradise, but not to heaven?

Paradise is not in heaven. Paradise is in hades. It is the region in hades referred to as the Bosom of Abraham. Remember, the Bosom of Abraham was the region of peace and safety within hades where righteous people were waiting for Jesus. That is where the thief was with Jesus immediately after their deaths.

18) Hell Is Eternal Judgment

The KJV further confuses the Christian's understanding of hell by declaring in Matthew 25:46 that punishment is "everlasting."

> *And these shall go away into everlasting punishment: but the righteous into life eternal.*
> (KJV)

The error in this verse becomes evident when we look more carefully at the words "everlasting" and "eternal." Both of these words have been translated from the Greek word, *aionion*. Yet, the KJV translators translated the same Greek word in two different ways within this one verse.

In contrast, most modern translations are consistent and, therefore, more honest in translating the Greek word *aionion*. For example, the NASV says (underlining added):

> *"These will go away into <u>eternal</u> punishment, but the righteous into <u>eternal</u> life."*
> (Matt. 25:46, NASV)

Notice that both times *aionion* is translated with the same word, "eternal."

Why did the KJV translators use the word "everlasting" to describe hell? They wanted to leave no question in the mind of the reader that hell entails everlasting pain and suffering. In reality, the original Greek manuscripts are not so clear on this issue. Please let me explain.

In Matthew 25:46, the word "punishment" is translated from the Greek word *kolasis*. This Greek word can be interpreted as punishment or as judgment. This means that Matthew 25:46 can be accurately translated by saying the wicked

Hell Is Eternal Judgment

with go away into "eternal judgment."

Eternal judgment is different than everlasting punishment. The second, everlasting punishment, entails ongoing pain, forever and ever. In contrast, eternal judgment can refer to God's final judgment, meaning the judgment from which there is no repentance, the judgment which will settle things eternally, once and for all.

The reason this distinction is important to understand is because there have been and are many Christian leaders who believe that the wicked people who will be thrown into hell will burn out of existence. They will not suffer in agony forever and forever. As Jesus said in Matthew 10:28 (NASV):

> "...fear Him [God] *who is able to destroy both soul and body in hell.*"

This view sees that God will put an end to the suffering of those cast into hell by totally annihilating them. They will be judged eternally, that is, finally.[4]

Whether hell entails forever pain or if it entails a final judgment which extinguishes people out of existence is not the main point. In fact, I do not want to lead you to one conclusion or the other. The point is that the translators of the KJV manipulated the translation of Matthew 25:46 so the reader is led to only one conclusion. The reader is not given the opportunity to decide for himself. In this sense the KJV is a commentary rather than a translation.

This is especially disturbing since the leaders of the Protestant Reformation claimed that they wanted to put the Bible into the language of the people so they could study and decide for themselves what the Bible teaches. Yet, in some Bible passages the KJV translators continued hiding from the readers

---

[4] For further teaching on this, see my book entitled *Hell, God's Justice, God's Mercy*.

what was actually being said. The readers are not allowed to decide for themselves when the translated words have been manipulated to lead to certain conclusions.

19) Women in the Ministry

Another mistake in the KJV can be seen in Roman 16:7 which says:

> Salute Andronicus and Junia, my kinsmen, and my fellowprisoners, who are of note among the apostles...

Notice the name "Junia." This is a man's name.

Yet, in the original Greek this is a name for a woman. The NASV maintains the proper gender translating it more accurately:

> Greet Andronicus and Junias, my kinsmen and my fellow prisoners, who are outstanding among the apostles...

This may seem like a small point to some readers, but it is very significant for those who want to understand how women were treated in ministry during the New Testament times. Junias was even mentioned among the apostles.

20) Isaiah 14 Is Not about Satan

Another misleading passage in the KJV is Isaiah 14:12:

> How art thou fallen from heaven, O Lucifer, son of the morning! how art thou cut down to the ground, which didst weaken the nations!

Isaiah 14 Is Not about Satan

In this verse, the word (or name) "Lucifer" has been added. This leads the reader to believe that this passage is about Satan.[5] But once a person learns that Lucifer is never mention in the original writings, it puts into question whether or not this passage should be used to develop a doctrine about Satan.

The historical origin of this word "Lucifer" is vague, but our earliest records show us that the Church Fathers Tertullian (ca. 160-220 AD)[6] and Origen (185-251 AD)[7] began associating Lucifer with Satan. However, it was not until the Fourth Century that Lucifer began to be used as the proper named for Satan. This primarily was the result of Jerome (347-420) inserting the name in the *Vulgate*, his Latin translation of the Bible, which was accepted as the common translation for the Roman Catholic Church from the Fifth to the Sixteenth Centuries. When the KJV was produced, the translators carried over this Latin name.

This is one of many passages which show us how the KJV translators borrowed from other translations. Modern proponents of the KJV like to say that the KJV was translated directly from the original manuscripts, but that simply is not true. Here in Isaiah 14:12, we find a word which is not even in the Hebrew manuscript, but was borrowed from the Latin *Vulgate*.

In Isaiah 14:12, there is a Hebrew word, *helel,* which is accurately translated "son of the morning" or "morning star." However, there is no justifiable reason to equate this with Lucifer or Satan. Therefore, most modern translations—Protestant and Roman Catholic—do not include Lucifer in this verse. The NASV says:

---

[5] In the margin of the first KJV of 1611, the translators commented that "O Lucifer" may also be understood as "O day-starre."

[6] *Contra Marrionem,* v.11, 17.

[7] *Ezekiel Opera,* iii. 356.

33

Living and Dying with the King James Bible

> *How you have fallen from heaven,*
> *O star of the morning, son of the dawn!*
> *You have been cut down to the earth,*
> *You who have weakened the nations!*
> (Is. 14:12, NASV)

Knowing that Lucifer is not mentioned in Isaiah 14, many great thinkers throughout Church history, including Martin Luther and John Calvin, attempted to break the unfounded teaching that Isaiah 14 was talking about Satan. Concerning the reference to Lucifer in Isaiah 14, Luther wrote, "This is not said of the angel who once was thrown out of heaven but of the king of Babylon, and it is figurative language."[8] Concerning the same passage, John Calvin wrote, "The exposition of this passage, which some have given, as if it referred to Satan, has arisen from ignorance; for the context plainly shows that these statements must be understood in reference to the king of the Babylonians."[9]

Unfortunately, the teaching that Isaiah 14 refers to Satan has become so deeply seated in Church tradition that it is difficult to successfully uproot.

Why is this important? Because the mistranslation in the KJV is used to teach the doctrine that Satan was once a good angel who led worship in heaven, but because of pride he was cast out of heaven. I do not mean to totally reject this doctrine. Perhaps it is true, but it is important to know that it cannot be developed unless one is using the KJV, and specifically a word in the KJV which was never in the original manuscripts.

Further confusion about Satan is introduced in the KJV because the translators made no distinction in the New Testament between devils and demons. In almost every case the Greek word *daimon* is translated as devil. In reality, there

---

[8] *Luther's Works,* vol. 16, p.140.
[9] *Commentary on Isaiah,* Volume First, p. 442.

Isaiah 14 Is Not about Satan

is only one devil mentioned in the original manuscripts, but there are many demons. Most modern translations reveal this distinction, while the KJV does not.

The end result of all these mistakes concerning Satan and demons is that readers of the KJV tend to overemphasize the role of Satan and demons in the world. They do not know they do this, because they have incorporated the whole KJV worldview into their system of thought. There tends to be among KJV advocates a concept of the universe being about a war between God and Satan. In reality, the universe is first and foremost about God raising up sons and daughters. Of course, there is a devil and there are demons, but they are not central to the message of the Bible. The Bible starts off in Genesis 1 with the story of how God created the universe and then created humanity in His own image. The Bible does *not* start off with the story of Satan being a good angel who fell. This is not to reject the story of Satan, but to focus on what the Bible focuses on.

This overemphasis on Satan can be seen in other KJV passages as well. For example, earlier I explained how the KJV translators mistranslated hades as hell. Hence, in Matthew 16:18, the words of Jesus are:

> ...*I will build my church; and the gates of hell shall not prevail against it.*

In the Middle Ages, hell was thought of as the realm of Satan, and therefore, this passage depicted a war between God and Satan.

In reality, Jesus said the gates of *hades* will not prevail against the Church. Hades is the place where dead people went. Hence, Jesus was declaring that the Church will not be overcome by death or the power of death. Indeed, the life of Jesus in the Church will overcome death.

More important is the general orientation of the KJV which leads to a form of Christianity which is too Satan and demon oriented. Of course, there is a devil and there are demons, but let me repeat that the world is not about a war between God and Satan. It is about God raising up sons and daughters who themselves will overcome death through the power of God.

21) The Holy Ghost Confusion in the KJV

The terminology "Holy Ghost" appears 89 times in the KJV. "Holy Spirit" appears seven. Yet, the word "ghost" and "spirit" are translated from the exact same Greek word, *pneuma*. Why did the KJV translators translate this Greek word in two different ways and why is this detrimental?

No modern translations—including the NKJV—use the terminology "Holy Ghost." One reason is because over the last century *ghost* has come to refer to the soul of a deceased person. Back in King James' times, *ghost* referred to an immaterial being, so it was appropriate then to use the word "Ghost" to refer to the Holy Spirit. Christians faithful to the KJV may continue being comfortable using the word "Ghost" but for those outside of those faithfuls the word is not easily associated with God's Spirit.

Another reason modern translators do not use the word "ghost" is because the word by itself does not refer to the Holy Spirit. The word "Holy" must be inserted before "Ghost" to identify the third Person of the Trinity. In contrast, the word "Spirit" can stand on its own and still refer to the third Person of the Trinity. Because "Ghost" cannot stand on its own, the KJV translators added the word "Holy" in some passages even though it was not in the original manuscripts.

The Holy Ghost Confusion in the KJV

This leads to further complications because whenever the KJV translators added the word "Holy," they were directing the reader to conclude that the Holy Spirit was being referred to. In reality, there are some Bible passages in which it is not clear if the writer is referring to the Holy Spirit, the breath of God, the spirit of man, or the spirit in the sense of being opposite of the flesh. For example, the KJV of I Corinthians 2:11-13 says:

> *For what man knoweth the things of a man, save the spirit of man which is in him? even so the things of God knoweth no man, but the Spirit of God. Now we have received, not the spirit of the world, but the spirit which is of God; that we might know the things that are freely given to us of God. Which things also we speak, not in the words which man's wisdom teacheth, but which the Holy Ghost teacheth...*

In this passage, the word "spirit" is used five times and "Holy Ghost" is used once, but all of these were translated from the Greek word *pneuma*. The KJV translators were careful scholars and they may have used the correct words in all of the appropriate places, but the reader is not allowed to know what the original writings actually said. The reader is not able to decide for himself or herself what "spirit" is being referred to.

In contrast, modern translators use the word "Spirit" so they do not have to decide if and when they should use the word "Ghost" and they do not have to add the word "Holy." Thus readers of more modern translations have a more accurate rendering of the original Greek manuscripts.

22) God Did Not Create Evil

The KJV translators made a more serious mistake when they translated the declaration of God in Isaiah 45:7 (underlining added):

> "I form the light, and create darkness:
> I make peace, and <u>create evil</u>..."

According to this verse, God creates evil.

Behind this word "evil" is the Hebrew word *rah*. In other passages of the KJV, *rah* is translated with other English words: calamity (Ps. 141:5); adversity (I Sam. 10:19); grievous (Prov. 15:10); sorrow (Gen. 44:29); trouble (Ps 27:5); distress (Nehemiah 2:17); affliction (II Chron. 20:9); misery (Eccl. 8:6); sore (Deut. 6:22); noisome (Ezek. 14:15); hurt (Gen. 26:29); and wretchedness (Num. 11:15).

It is unfortunate that the KJV translators used the word "evil" in Isaiah 45:7, because it credits God with creating evil. Typically theologians will say that everything God created is good, but Satan and humanity corrupted God's good creation. Hence, God did not create evil, but He created the opportunity for evil to come into existence.

Not only is the KJV of Isaiah 47:7 a misleading translation, but it is not consistent with the contrast being made in the passage. Look again at how the passage is making contrasts (underlining added):

> "I form the <u>light</u>, and create <u>darkness</u>:
> I make <u>peace</u>, and create <u>evil</u>..."

Light is the opposite of darkness, but peace is *not* the opposite of evil. A better contrast is made in the NASV (underlining added):

*The One forming <u>light</u> and creating <u>darkness</u>,
Causing <u>well-being</u> and creating <u>calamity</u>;*

Just like light is the opposite of darkness, so well-being is the opposite of calamity.

Why is this important? Because the KJV distorts our concept of God. He does not create evil.

23) God Is Spirit

A further distortion about God's nature has resulted from how the KJV translators added the indefinite article "a" right before the word "Spirit," in John 4:24:[10]

"God is a Spirit..."

More accurate translations like the NASV tell us:

"God is spirit..."

Before I explain why this difference is significant, let me point out that the *New World Translation*, which is the official version used by the Jehovah Witnesses, makes a similar error by inserting the indefinite article, "a" right before the word, "god" in John 1:1. Because of this error, the Jehovah Witnesses say that the Word is merely "a" god, rather than God.

The KJV translators similarly inserted the indefinite article "a" in John 4:24, which leads the reader to conclude that God is "a Spirit." Many Christians have taken this to mean that God has no other aspects to His nature other than "a Spirit." In reality, there are many verses which refer to God's soul. For example, in Hebrews 10:38 (NASV) we read God

---

[10] The NKJV corrected this error.

saying:

> But My righteous One shall live by faith;
> And if he shrinks back, My soul has no pleasure in him.

From verses like this we can conclude that God has a soul. Therefore, He is not just "a spirit."

This stirs inquisitive minds to go back to John 4:24 and research where the KJV translators went wrong. What we find is that the original Greek manuscripts of the New Testament say that God is spirit (not a spirit). This word, "spirit," was being used in the context of Jesus talking to a Samaritan woman. She asked Jesus where people should worship God, on the Samaritan holy mountain or in the Jewish temple in Jerusalem. Jesus answered by saying the location is not important because God is not limited to the natural realm—God is spirit, in the sense that God exists in the spiritual realm.

Rather than seeing God as "a Spirit," we should see that God is "spirit," having no natural substance to His being. He is spiritual. Hence, we can understand how God can have both a soul and a spirit which both exist in the spiritual realm.

24) Man Is Not "a Spirit"

Some Christian groups have taken the mistranslation in the KJV of John 4:24 (which we just looked at) and developed some misunderstandings about the nature of humanity. Their thought processes usually align with the following path:

> 1) God is "a Spirit," (from the KJV)
> 2) Man is created in the image of God,
> 3) Therefore, man is "a spirit."

I hope you can see the fallacy of this argument. It starts off with the false idea that God is "a Spirit." As soon as we discard that error we realize there is no basis for the argument. Then we can look more carefully in the Bible and find many passages which refer to man's body, soul and spirit. More importantly, when Adam was created he *"became a living soul"* (Gen. 2:7, KJV). Therefore, it is wrong to say that man is "a spirit."

The idea that man is a spirit has led to many wrong and even bizarre doctrines, based on a mystical, rather than a wholistic understanding of human nature. By wholistic, I mean an understanding which incorporates the entirety of a person's being, including body, soul and spirit. Please do not dismiss such mistakes as minor errors. The implications are so numerous I have written extensively about this in another book, *The Spiritual, the Mystical and the Supernatural.*

The KJV leads to more confusion about the nature of humanity by mistranslating Psalm 8:5:

For thou hast made him a little lower than the angels, and hast crowned him with glory and honour.

Notice that man is said to be created a *little lower than the angels*. In reality, the word "angels" in this verse is translated from the Hebrew word *Elohim*, which actually means "gods" or "God." A correct translation of Psalm 8:5 (NASV) is:

Yet You have made him a little lower than God,
And You crown him with glory and majesty!

Contrary to what the KJV leads us to believe, angels are not of a higher order than humanity. I Corinthians 6:3 says that we will judge the angels on judgment day. We are higher than angels, but a little lower than God. People, not angels, are created in the image of God.

25) Animals Have Souls

The KJV not only leads to misunderstandings about the nature of humanity, the nature of God and the nature of Satan, but also about the nature of animals. Several verses in the KJV tell us that the life of animals is in their blood (i.e., Lev. 17:11, 14). The Hebrew word translated as "life" is *nephesh*, which actually means "soul." Therefore, the original writings say that the soul of the animal is in the blood.

This leads us to conclude that animals have a soul. This does not mean they have an eternal soul. Nor does it mean that the souls of animals are the same as the souls of humans. We know that Adam's soul came into existence as God breathed His Spirit into Adam's body. Animals were not created in this fashion. Their souls are neither eternal nor created in the image of God.

However, animals do have souls. They have the ability to bond and have relationships. They have some invisible side to their nature.

This changes how we look at animals. In the Middle Ages and during the Protestant Reformation, animals were thought of as creatures of instinct, having no will or personality. In keeping with that understanding, Church leaders were comfortable saying that animals have life, but they were not comfortable saying that animals have a soul. Hence, they changed the meaning intended by the original Bible writers.

It was not only the KJV translators who have done this, but several modern translators followed in making this error. This is one example of how the KJV has carried so much weight historically that it has influenced and even dominated how some of the more modern Bible translators have worded certain passages.

26) "The" Root of All Evil

Another mistake in the KJV is in I Timothy 6:10, which says:

> *For the love of money is the root of all evil...*

The definite article, "the" right before "root" is not in the original Greek. It was added by the KJV translators. As a result, some teachers have used this error over the last 400 years to single out the love of money as the worse sin of all. In reality, the love of money is *a* root of all evil.

Carelessness in inserting the definite article can be seen in other passages, as well. The KJV of Romans 12:3 ends by saying:

> *...according as God hath dealt to every man the measure of faith.*

The definite article, "the" right before "measure" is not in the original Greek. Better translations such as the NASV translate these same words more accurately:

> *...as God has allotted to each a measure of faith.*

The reason this is important to note is because some modern Christian groups which use only the KJV have developed a teaching which says that every person has been given *"the* measure of faith," implying that every person has the exact same amount of faith given to them by God. Building on this misunderstanding, those Christian groups teach that everyone has the same faith, but the only difference between one person and another is how much they use that faith.

That may seem like a small point, but it becomes a significant issue when someone who is physically sick is told

43

that they are being lazy and not using *the* faith which God gave them. On the positive side, this teaching can be used to encourage everyone to use their faith and believe God. On the negative side, the teaching can be used to make the sick individual feel condemned and like a failure.

Whether the teaching is used for good or bad, it is based on one word, "the," which is not even in the original Greek manuscripts.

27) Does Not Allow for Ongoing Research

The example just discussed reveals a serious problem with the KJV. The KJV translators had no way of knowing how the insertion of one word, "the," would be misused years later. Those Seventeenth-Century translators were especially careful in interpreting verses which dealt with issues important during their time in history. On the other hand, there are issues which have confronted the Church over the last four hundred years which the KJV scholars never had to face.

As the years go by, new challenges arise. As false teachings develop, serious Bible students are motivated to research and more accurately translate every word from the Greek and Hebrew manuscripts. New challenges demand further study. Only if we are willing to correct errors made in earlier translations can we deal with the challenges of the present and future. In other words, time proves the integrity of any Bible translation, and the advocates of the original KJV have refused to face the tests which time has brought.

28) The Trinitarian Statement in the KJV

Advocates of the KJV will sometimes remain loyal to their favorite version because they have been taught that the KJV

The Trinitarian Statement in the KJV

supports the Trinity more than any other Bible version. This is because the KJV of I John 5:7-8, has a "trinitarian statement," which is a statement which supports the doctrine of the Trinity (the statement consists of the underlined words):

> *For there are three that <u>bear record in heaven, the Father, the Word, and the Holy Ghost: and these three are one. And there are three that</u> bear witness in earth, the Spirit, and the water, and the blood: and these three agree in one.*

In contrast, the NASV says:

> *For there are three that testify: the Spirit and the water and the blood; and the three are in agreement.*

The NIV is exactly the same as the NASV (with the addition of one comma):

> *For there are three that testify: the Spirit, and the water and the blood; and the three are in agreement.*

Why does the KJV have the extra wording? Is this wording a reason to use the KJV rather than other translations? As I answer these questions, please don't misunderstand me. I believe in the Trinity. I believe there are three Persons in One God. There are many passages in the Bible which reveal this to us. I point this out because we should not justify clinging to the KJV just because it supports a doctrine which we believe. The only reason we should cling to a certain Bible version is because it is an accurate translation of what God had the original authors write.

So was the trinitarian statement in the original writings? The evidence tells us that it was not.

When Erasmus first published the *Textus Receptus* in 1516, he did not include the trinitarian statement because he could not find it in any Greek manuscript. However, the statement was in later versions (after the Eighth Century) of the Latin *Vulgate*, so Roman Catholics, who were loyal to the *Vulgate*, complained that Erasmus did not include it in his Greek text. Erasmus responded in the annotations of his second edition of the *Textus Receptus*, explaining that he could not find it in any Greek manuscript.

In 1520, a scribe named Roy provided Erasmus with a Greek text having the extra words. Therefore, Erasmus added the statement in his third edition of the *Textus Receptus*, published in 1522. To date, only four Greek manuscripts have been found which have the trinitarian statement, and all four date from the Sixteenth Century or later. No early manuscripts in Greek or Latin have this statement.

Evidence that the trinitarian statement of I John 5 was not in the original manuscripts is the fact that none of the early Church fathers quoted from this passage. As I mentioned earlier, we have their writings which quoted more than 80,000 verses from the New Testament. How is it possible that they never quoted these words? This is especially significant because the doctrine of the Trinity was probably the most debated issue of the first five centuries. If the trinitarian statement had been available to the Bible teachers of the time, they certainly would have used it to establish their position. But they didn't. The most logical conclusion is that the trinitarian statement was not in the original writings.

While KJV advocates cling to the added trinitarian statement of I John 5, they miss equally key passages which would have supported the Trinity if the KJV had been translated more accurately. For example, the KJV of Titus 2:13 says:

Why Is All of This Important?

Looking for that blessed hope, and the glorious appearing of the great God and our Saviour Jesus Christ;

In contrast, the NASV says:

looking for the blessed hope and the appearing of the glory of our great God and Savior, Christ Jesus,

Notice that the KJV inserted the word "our" right before "Saviour Jesus Christ."[11] This allows the reader to see "our great God" as separate from "our Savior Christ Jesus." In contrast, the NASV reads so as to make it clear that our great God is the Savior Christ Jesus. Most importantly, the NASV has translated this verse as it was in the Greek manuscripts, while the KJV did not translate this correctly.

29) Why Is All of This Important?

Even though I have pointed out all of these errors in the KJV (and there are others), some readers may respond by saying, "So what?" They may not think that any of these errors are important enough for us fuss. They think they can "eat the meat and spit out the bones." Please reconsider.

Think again about the errors which I mentioned concerning how the KJV promotes the institutional Church and authoritarian government. The corresponding words were used because the translators knew that they would have a certain impact upon the readers. Words such as "Church," "Bishop," and "ruling over" have a profound impact upon people who take the Bible to be God's Word (people like me).

---

[11] The NKJV corrected this error.

Living and Dying with the King James Bible

The truth sets free and lies put people in bondage.

I am concerned for the Christian who is not upset at the errors made in the KJV. If you think it is no big deal that the KJV uses words which are more authoritarian than the Bible writers intended, then perhaps it is because you have become accustomed to a form of Christianity which is more authoritarian than God intends. If you are comfortable with a Bible translation that is condemning and over-exaggerates the wickedness of humanity, perhaps it is because you have a worldview which is condemning and sees people as more evil than they really are. If the communication of untruths does not upset you, it may be because you have embraced those untruths and you have fully incorporated them into your thought patterns.

Those thought patterns include distortions in our understanding of God, the Holy Spirit, the Church, humanity, Satan, demons, animals, hell, hades, paradise, eternity and the victorious Christian life. These issues are not minor. They are central to Christianity.

My concerns go beyond these issues. For over 25 years, I have been traveling the world, teaching in churches, conferences and Bible schools. I have repeatedly encountered Christians who will not change in some specific area, and sometimes the reason they will not change is because their KJV taught them to think a certain way—a way that is wrong. Their unquestioned loyalty to the KJV is keeping them from considering any new ideas or ways of understanding the Scriptures. Of course, any Christian can stubbornly hold onto cherished beliefs, but I have found such stubbornness more frequently among KJV loyalists. I am sorry to say this if you are a KJV loyalist, but it is what I have found to be true. It is an unwillingness to change that concerns me.

30) Unreadable to the Modern Mind

Finally, the KJV is difficult to understand for most modern people. Since 1611, when it was first produced, the KJV has been revised to keep up with some adaptations to more modern terminology, but it is still built on the Old English grammar which becomes more and more difficult to understand as people move further away from the language spoken in the Seventeenth Century.[12]

The NKJV got rid of the Thee's and Thou's and some other outdated terms, but the bulk of the message remains in a language which is difficult for most modern readers.

Of course, KJV and NKJV loyalists will object because they were raised hearing the Old English. But that is the point. We need a version that is understandable to non-Christians, non-churched people and new Christians. We shouldn't orient our ministry toward ourselves. Our goal is to reach the lost and feed others.

This is especially important for leaders. If a leader is using the KJV, then the people who follow him or her are likely to use the KJV. Perhaps the leader can easily understand the old English terminology because of years and years of use, but they should not expect their younger disciples to understand it. In some cases the leader may unknowingly be chaining their disciples to a Bible translation which they cannot fully understand.

This is most obvious in countries outside of the Western world. Having spent many years traveling around the world, I have met thousands of Christians for whom English is not their first language, and with English as their second or third language, they are finding it extremely difficult to understand the Old English which is used in the KJV and NKJV.

---

[12] For a list of 419 archiac words used in the KJV see: http://www.bible.ca/b-kjv-only.htm#errors

Living and Dying with the King James Bible

It is even hard for modern people in the Western world to understand. To realize how foreign the Old English is to modern people—especially young people—check out how many high school students are willingly enrolling in Shakespeare classes today. When my youngest son was in high school, that was the one class he complained about more than any other. One in fifty students may enjoy untangling the Shakespearian phraseology, but the vast majority will only endure the class because it is required. Very few will ever again pick up a writing of Shakespeare on their own initiative.

So why would the average business traveler spend his or her leisure time laboring through the KJV which has been left in a motel by the Gideon Association? It would be much easier to turn on the television which has been formatted and designed for effective communication. Television marketers have spent millions learning how to communicate their message and it seems obvious that they know what they are doing. From my acquaintance with the Gideons, it seems that the average age of the active members is over sixty years old. God bless them for their faithfulness, but if they are trying to reach the lost, they should at the very least learn from modern advertisers. Or they can learn from William Tyndale, John Wycliffe, Martin Luther or John Calvin who risked their lives to put the Bible in a language which the common people could understand.

Conclusion

Perhaps the KJV is understandable to you. Maybe you have memorized dozens or even hundreds of verses in the KJV. But your use of this version may be influencing others to use a translation which is hindering *them* from reading and clearly understanding the Word of God. If you dare to admit it, the KJV may also be hindering you in your walk with God.

I don't say this to make you mad. I say this because I love the Church and have given my life to helping the Church. I am a teacher. I have founded a dozen Bible Colleges in other nations. I have spent my adult life teaching the Bible at churches and schools around the world. More importantly, my heart is wholly directed toward helping the Church succeed and I know that the KJV is a stumbling block to the Church's advancement. It is holding devout believers in many errors of the Sixteenth Century. That breaks my heart.

I am not asking you to destroy your KJV, nor even get rid of it. You can keep your treasure as a reference and even pull it out from time to time if you want to bathe in the grandeur of its language. But there are many modern translations which put the Words of God more accurately in your hands.

Other Books by Harold R. Eberle

Christianity Unshackled

Most Christians in the Western world have no idea how profoundly their beliefs have been influenced by their culture. What would Christianity be like, if it was separated from Western thought? After untangling the Western traditions of the last 2,000 years of Church history, Harold R. Eberle offers a Christian worldview that is clear, concise, and liberating. This will shake you to the core and then leave you standing on a firm foundation!

Compassionate Capitalism:
A Judeo-Christian Value

This book is a look into history to see where and how capitalism was born and developed through the centuries. As you read this book, you will learn how capitalism first developed as God worked among the Hebrew people in the Old Testament. The resulting economic principles then transformed Western society as they spread with Christianity. What remains is for us to apply the principles of capitalism with compassion.

Releasing Kings into the Marketplace for Ministry
By John Garfield and Harold R. Eberle

"Kings" is what we call Christian leaders who have embraced the call of God upon their life to work in the marketplace and from that position transform society. This book explains how marketplace ministry will operate in concert with local churches and pastors. It provides a Scriptural basis for the expansion of the Kingdom of God into all areas of society.

Other Books by Harold R. Eberle

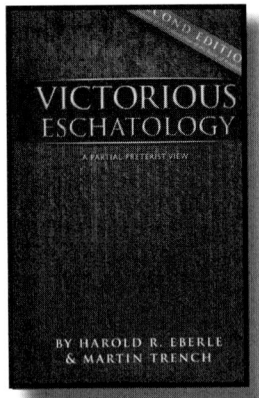

Victorious Eschatology
Co-authored by
Harold R. Eberle and Martin Trench

Here it is—a biblically-based, optimistic view of the future. Along with a historical perspective, this book offers a clear understanding of Matthew 24, the book of Revelation, and other key passages about the events to precede the return of Jesus Christ. Satan is not going to take over this world. Jesus Christ is Lord and He will reign until every enemy is put under His feet!

Jesus Came Out of the Tomb...So Can You!
A Brief Explanation of Resurrection-based Christianity

Forgiveness of sins is at the cross. Power over sin is in the resurrection and ascension. Unfortunately, too many Christians have only benefited from the death of Jesus and not His life. If God raised Jesus from the tomb in power and glory, then we can experience that resurrection power. If God raised Jesus into heaven, and us with Him, then we can live in His victory!

Developing a Prosperous Soul
Vol. I: How to Overcome a Poverty Mind-set
Vol. II: How to Move into God's Financial Blessings

There are fundamental changes you can make in the way you think which will help you release God's blessings. This is a balanced look at the promises of God with practical steps you can take to move into financial freedom. It is time for Christians to recapture the financial arena. These two volumes will inspire and create faith in you to fulfill God's purpose for your life.

Other Books by Harold R. Eberle

The Spiritual, Mystical, and Supernatural

The first five volumes of Harold R. Eberle's series of books entitled, *Spiritual Realities,* have been condensed into this one volume, 372 pages in length. Topics are addressed such as how the spiritual and natural worlds are related, angelic and demonic manifestations, signs and wonders, miracles and healing, the anointing, good versus evil spiritual practices, how people are created by God to access the spiritual realm, how the spirits of people interact, how people sense things in the spirit realm, and much more.

The Complete Wineskin
(Fourth edition)

The Body of Christ is in a reformation. God is pouring out His Holy Spirit and our wineskins must be changed to handle the new wine. Will the Church come together in unity? How does the anointing of God work and what is your role? What is the 5-fold ministry? How are apostles, prophets, evangelists, pastors, and teachers going to rise up and work together? Where do small group meetings fit in? This book puts into words what you have been sensing in your spirit. (Eberle's best seller, translated into many languages, distributed worldwide.)

God's Leaders for Tomorrow's World
(Revised/expanded edition)

You sense the call to leadership, but questions persist: "Does God want me to rise up? Do I truly know where to lead? Is this pride? How can I influence people?" Through an understanding of leadership dynamics, learn how to develop godly charisma. Confusion will melt into order when you see the God-ordained lines of authority. Fear of leadership will change to confidence as you learn to handle power struggles. It is time to move into your "metron," that is, your God-given sphere of authority.

Other Books by Harold R. Eberle

Who Is God?

Challenging the traditional Western view of God, Harold R. Eberle presents God as a Covenant-maker, Lover, and Father. Depending on Scripture, God is shown to be in a vulnerable, open, and cooperative relationship with His people. This book is both unsettling and enlightening—revolutionary to most readers—considered by many to be Harold's most important contribution to the Body of Christ.

Grace...the Power to Reign
The Light Shining from Romans 5-8

We struggle against sin and yearn for God's highest. Yet, on a bad day it is as if we are fighting against gravity. Questions go unanswered:

- Where is the power to overcome temptations and trials?
- Is God really willing to breathe into us that these dry bones can live and we may stand strong?

For anyone who has ever struggled to live godly, here are the answers.

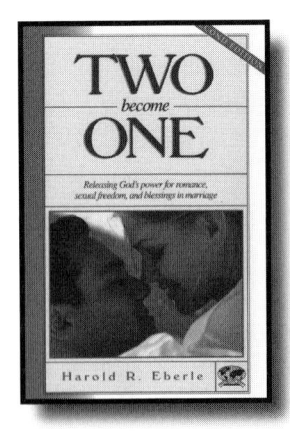

Two Become One
(Second edition)
Releasing God's Power for Romance, Sexual Freedom and Blessings in Marriage

The keys to a thrilling, passionate, and fulfilling marriage can be yours if you want them. Kindle afresh the "buzz of love." Find out how to make God's law of binding forces work for you rather than against you. This book is of great benefit to pastors, counselors, young singles, divorces, and especially married people. Couples are encouraged to read it together.

To place an order or to check current prices on these and other books, call:

1-800-308-5837 within the USA or
509-248-5837 from outside of the USA

Worldcast Publishing
P.O. Box 10653
Yakima, WA 98909-1653

E-mail: office@worldcastpublishing.com
Web Site: www.worldcastpublishing.com